Made in United States
Troutdale, OR
12/12/2023

15760324R00072